Gra
good news

Michael and Joanne Cole

Blackie

There was always something for Gran to grumble about.
Today it was the television.
"There's nothing good on it," she said.

“I’m sick and tired of old cowboy films,” she said, and switched over to the other side.

Then came the news. It wasn't good.
"I'm fed up with bad news," said Gran,
and switched over.

The weather forecast was on the other channel.
It was bad.
"Thunderstorms in all areas," said the announcer.

"Then you must find some good news," said a voice.
The voice seemed to belong to a rabbit.

But it wasn't a rabbit. It was her grandson Jim who had come to visit her.
"I've got some news," he said.

"I'm playing the part of a rabbit in the school play. Will you help me with my costume?"

Gran put the finishing touches to his costume
and made him a tail from an old powder puff.
"Good luck," she said.

In the play Jim was the first to appear on stage.
The audience clapped him.

It was a long time before the clapping stopped and he could go off. He was the last on, too.

He got a lot more clapping from the audience.

When Jim got home, the first thing he did was to switch on the television. He hadn't watched it for a long time.

A familiar face appeared on the screen. It was Gran with a new hat.
"This is the Gran o'clock News," said Gran.

"Although the rain has caused flooding here, the sunshine in Spain is making the oranges sweet and juicy."

"And in the zoo – at last – a baby panda has been born. And that's not all the good news."

"Later on you can see a brand new cowboy film
called 'Gran Gets her Man'."

"Goodness me!" said Jim. "Gran's a star. I must get her to sign my autograph book."

Then, stopping to get some flowers on the way,
he hurried to see Gran.

"You're lucky to find me in," said Gran, when Jim arrived. She was trying on a new hat.

“I’ve been busy since I took your advice about finding good news, and I started my Good News programme.”

The telephone rang.
"Yes," said Gran, "I can manage tomorrow. Goodbye. They want me to star in another programme," she said to Jim.

"The only trouble is," she said, signing her autograph, "that I've no time to watch television – and now there are some good programmes on it."

First published in 1983 by Blackie and Son Limited

British Library Cataloguing in Publication Data

Cole, Joanne
Gran's good news. – (Gran)
I. Title II. Cole, Michael, *1933–*
823′.914 [J] PZ7

ISBN 0-216-91280-6
ISBN 0-216-91281-4 Pbk

Blackie and Son Limited
A Member of the Blackie Group
Furnival House, 14-18 High Holborn, London WC1V 6BX

Printed by Cambus Litho, East Kilbride, Scotland.